A
Betty Crocker
PICTURE COOKBOOK
Quick-to-Fix
Mainstays

D0036643

GOLDEN PRESS/NEW YORK
Western Publishing Company, Inc.
Racine, Wisconsin

Library of Congress Catalog Card Number: 81-83383
ISBN 0-307-09670-X

Golden® and Golden Press® are trademarks of
Western Publishing Company, Inc.

CONTENTS

Beef

Pork

To save time, slice several celery stalks together.

Toast nuts in 350° oven until golden, 10 to 15 minutes.

Hamburger Chop Suey

1 pound ground beef
1 medium onion, sliced
2 large stalks celery, sliced (about 1½ cups)
1 tablespoon instant beef bouillon
2 cups hot water
¼ cup cold water
3 tablespoons soy sauce
2 tablespoons cornstarch
¼ teaspoon monosodium glutamate
1 can (16 ounces) bean sprouts, drained
1 can (8 ounces) water chestnuts, drained
   and sliced
4 cups hot cooked rice
½ cup slivered almonds or chopped cocktail
   peanuts, toasted (see note)
1 jar (2 ounces) sliced pimiento, drained

Cook and stir ground beef over medium heat in 10-inch skillet until light brown; drain. Stir in onion, celery, instant bouillon and hot water. Heat to boiling; reduce heat.

Shake cold water, soy sauce, cornstarch and monosodium glutamate in tightly covered container. Stir into beef mixture. Heat to boiling, stirring constantly. Boil and stir 1 minute. Stir in bean sprouts and water chestnuts; heat until water chestnuts are hot. Serve over rice. Garnish with toasted almonds and pimiento.   6 SERVINGS.

Note: To toast almonds, spread on ungreased baking sheet and bake in 350° oven, stirring occasionally, until golden, 10 to 15 minutes.

Cook and stir over low heat.

Break up tomatoes with fork.

Beef-Rice Creole

1 pound ground beef
1 tablespoon flour
2 teaspoons salt
½ medium green pepper, chopped (about
   ½ cup)
1 small onion, chopped (about ¼ cup)
2 tablespoons snipped parsley
¼ teaspoon pepper
⅛ teaspoon red pepper sauce (optional)
1 clove garlic, finely chopped
1 bay leaf
  Dash of ground thyme
1½ cups water
1 can (8 ounces) whole tomatoes
1½ cups uncooked instant rice

Cook and stir ground beef in 10-inch skillet until light brown; drain. Sprinkle beef with flour and salt. Stir in green pepper, onion, parsley, pepper, pepper sauce, garlic, bay leaf and thyme. Cook and stir over low heat until onion is tender, about 5 minutes.

Stir water and tomatoes (with liquid) into beef mixture; break up tomatoes with fork. Heat to boiling; reduce heat. Cover and simmer 5 minutes. Stir in rice; remove from heat. Cover and let stand 5 minutes.   4 SERVINGS.

GROUND BEEF varies in fat content, shrinkage and price. Regular ground beef (top left), budget priced, has 20 to 25% fat and will shrink during cooking. Ground chuck (top right), medium priced, has 15 to 20% fat and will shrink less. Ground round (bottom), at a higher price, has 11% fat, so there is little cooking shrinkage.

Mexican-Style Skillet Supper

- 1 pound ground beef
- 1 teaspoon salt
- ⅛ teaspoon pepper
- 10 ounces Cheddar cheese, cubed (about 2 cups)
- 2 medium stalks celery, sliced (about 1 cup)
- ⅓ cup sliced pitted ripe olives
- 1 package (7 ounces) main dish mix for beef noodle
- 1 can (16 ounces) stewed tomatoes
- 1 teaspoon chili powder (optional)
- ¾ cup water

Cook and stir ground beef in 10-inch skillet over medium heat until light brown; drain. Sprinkle beef with salt and pepper. Layer half each of the cheese, celery, olives and half of the Noodles from main dish mix package on beef; repeat.

Blend tomatoes, Sauce Mix from main dish mix package and chili powder; stir in water. Pour tomato mixture on noodles in skillet. Heat to boiling; reduce heat. Cover and simmer until noodles are tender, about 10 minutes.

6 SERVINGS.

Taco Submarines

2 packages (10 ounces each) brown and
   serve French-style rolls (6 inches long)
1 pound ground beef
½ cup dairy sour cream
¼ cup water
1 package (1¼ ounces) taco seasoning mix
   Mayonnaise or salad dressing
   Shredded lettuce
6 slices Swiss cheese, cut diagonally in half
3 medium tomatoes, each cut into 4 slices

Bake rolls as directed on package. Cook and stir ground
beef in 10-inch skillet over medium heat until light brown;
drain. Stir in sour cream, water and seasoning mix; reduce
heat. Simmer uncovered 5 minutes.

Cut rolls in half; spread with mayonnaise. Place lettuce on
bottoms. Layer about ⅓ cup beef mixture, 2 cheese slices
and 2 tomato slices on each sandwich. Cover with top of
roll; secure with wooden pick.   6 SUBMARINES.

Stir sour cream, water and
taco seasoning mix into beef.

Layer beef mixture, 2 cheese
and 2 tomato slices on rolls.

Start rice while beef browns.   Let rice stand; slice tomatoes.

Add water to pineapple syrup.   Stir sugar mixture into beef.

Sweet-Sour Beef with Rice

```
 1  pound ground beef
 1  medium onion, sliced
1½  cups water
 2  teaspoons butter or margarine (optional)
 ½  teaspoon salt
1½  cups uncooked instant rice
 ⅓  cup packed brown sugar
 2  tablespoons cornstarch
 ¼  cup cider vinegar
 3  tablespoons soy sauce
 1  can (13½ ounces) pineapple tidbits,
        drained (reserve syrup)
 1  can (16 ounces) chow mein vegetables,
        drained
    Sliced tomatoes
```

Cook and stir ground beef and onion in 10-inch skillet until beef is light brown; drain. Heat water, butter and salt to boiling in 2-quart saucepan. Stir in rice; remove from heat. Cover and let stand 5 minutes.

Mix brown sugar, cornstarch, vinegar and soy sauce. Add enough water to reserved pineapple syrup to measure 1 cup; stir into sugar mixture. Stir sugar mixture into beef and onion. Heat to boiling; reduce heat. Cook, stirring constantly, until thickened. Stir in pineapple and chow mein vegetables. Heat until vegetables are hot. Fluff rice with fork. Serve beef with rice. Garnish with tomatoes.

4 SERVINGS.

Beef and Biscuit Casseroles

1 pound ground beef
1 medium onion, chopped (about ½ cup)
½ small green pepper, chopped (about
 ¼ cup)
1 can (8 ounces) tomato sauce
1 can (4½ ounces) chopped pitted ripe
 olives
¼ cup water
1 teaspoon salt
1 teaspoon chili powder
 Biscuit Topping (right)

Heat oven to 425°. Cook and stir ground beef in 10-inch skillet until light brown; stir in onion and green pepper. Cook until beef is brown; drain. Stir in tomato sauce, olives, water, salt and chili powder. Divide beef mixture among 4 ungreased 10-ounce baking dishes.

Prepare Biscuit Topping; drop dough by teaspoonfuls onto beef mixture. Bake until Biscuit Topping is golden brown, about 15 minutes.   4 SERVINGS.

BISCUIT TOPPING
Mix 1 cup biscuit baking mix, ¼ cup shredded Cheddar cheese and ¼ cup cold water until a soft dough forms; beat vigorously 20 strokes.

Chop onion and green pepper while ground beef browns.

Measure the ingredients for the biscuits and reserve.

Drop dough by teaspoonfuls onto beef mixture in dishes.

Place dishes on baking sheet; bake until golden brown.

Meatballs on Crisp Noodles

1 pound ground beef
2 tablespoons soy sauce
½ teaspoon ground ginger
1½ cups water
2 tablespoons cornstarch
2 packages (6 ounces each) frozen pea
    pods
1 small red pepper, cut into 1x¼-inch
    pieces (about ½ cup)
1 teaspoon instant beef bouillon
¾ teaspoon salt
    Chow mein noodles

Mix ground beef, soy sauce and ginger. Shape by rounded tablespoonfuls into balls. Cook and stir meatballs in 10-inch skillet over medium heat until brown, about 15 minutes; drain.

Mix water and cornstarch. Rinse frozen pea pods under running cold water to separate; drain. Stir cornstarch mixture, pea pods, red pepper, instant bouillon and salt into meatballs. Heat to boiling; boil and stir 1 minute. Serve over chow mein noodles.   4 SERVINGS.

KITCHEN AIDS

Your ice-cream scoop is a most versatile and time-saving utensil. Use it for shaping meatballs and croquettes (and placing them in the skillet); for measuring cupcake, muffin, pancake and fritter batters and for serving mashed potatoes, stuffing, rice and cottage cheese. The number on the scoop tells how many scoops in a quart. (The #6 scoop equals ⅔ cup, the #40 scoop equals 1 3/5 tablespoons.)

Mushroom Steak

6 to 8 beef cubed steaks (about 2 pounds)
2 teaspoons salt
¼ teaspoon lemon pepper
2 cans (4 ounces each) sliced mushrooms
½ cup dry white or red wine
1 medium green pepper, chopped (½ cup)
1 small onion, chopped (about ¼ cup)

Sprinkle steaks with salt and lemon pepper. Brown few steaks at a time in 10-inch skillet over medium heat, 5 to 10 minutes on each side. Stir in mushrooms (with liquid), wine, green pepper and onion. Heat over low heat until mushrooms are hot, about 5 minutes.   6 TO 8 SERVINGS.

Beef Scramble

12 eggs, beaten
1 jar (2½ ounces) dried beef, cut into thin
    strips
1 cup creamed cottage cheese
¼ cup snipped green onion tops or chives
¼ cup butter or margarine

Mix eggs, dried beef and cheese. (At this point, mixture can be refrigerated up to 24 hours.)

Cook and stir onion tops in butter in 10-inch skillet over low heat until tender, 2 to 3 minutes. Stir in egg mixture. As mixture thickens, gently lift cooked portion with spatula so thin uncooked portion can flow to bottom. Avoid constant stirring. Cook until eggs are thickened but still moist, about 15 minutes.   8 SERVINGS.

Busy Day Stew

1 large onion, sliced
1 jar (5 ounces) dried beef, cut up
3 tablespoons vegetable oil
2 tablespoons flour
1 teaspoon instant beef bouillon
¼ teaspoon pepper
1½ cups water
1 jar (16 ounces) whole carrots, drained
1 can (16 ounces) whole new potatoes, drained

Cook and stir onion and beef in oil in 2-quart saucepan over medium heat until onion is brown. Stir in remaining ingredients. Heat to boiling, stirring constantly; reduce heat. Cover and simmer 5 minutes.   4 OR 5 SERVINGS.

Beef-Rice Cakes

1 cup uncooked brown rice
3 eggs, slightly beaten
1 cup shredded Swiss cheese (about 4 ounces)
1 package (3 ounces) sliced smoked beef, cut up
¾ teaspoon onion salt

Cook rice as directed on package. Heat lightly greased griddle to 400°. Mix rice and remaining ingredients. Drop by ½ cupfuls onto hot griddle. Cook until edges are light brown, about 3 minutes. Turn and cook 2 minutes.
8 CAKES.

Avocado Chili

Parmesan Fingers (below)
2 medium avocados
1 can (40 ounces) chili with beans
⅛ teaspoon garlic powder
⅛ teaspoon chili powder

Prepare Parmesan Fingers. Peel avocados; cut lengthwise in half and remove pits. Place avocado halves in individual serving bowls.

Heat chili, garlic powder and chili powder over low heat until chili is hot. Spoon chili into avocados. Serve with Parmesan Fingers.   4 SERVINGS.

PARMESAN FINGERS

Heat oven to 400°. Separate dough from 1 package (11 ounces) refrigerated baking powder biscuits; cut each biscuit in half. Shape halves into ropes 3 inches long. Place rolls on ungreased baking sheet. Brush with ¼ cup butter or margarine, melted; sprinkle with ¼ cup grated Parmesan cheese. Bake until golden brown, 10 to 12 minutes.

Toss mixture of milk, onion, horseradish and salt with pota-to-hash-beet mixture.

Spread in melted shortening in skillet. Cook until bottom is brown. Add onions; bake.

Yankee Hash-Onion Bake

1 can (16 ounces) whole new potatoes, drained and finely chopped
1 can (15 ounces) corned beef hash, finely chopped
1 can (8¼ ounces) sliced beets, drained and finely chopped
3 tablespoons milk
1 teaspoon instant minced onion
1 teaspoon prepared horseradish
½ teaspoon salt
3 tablespoons shortening
1 can (3 ounces) French fried onions
Eggs Sunny-Side Up (right)

Toss potatoes, hash and beets. Mix milk, onion, horserad-ish and salt; let stand 3 minutes. Toss with hash mixture.

Heat oven to 350°. Heat shortening in 10-inch ovenproof skillet until melted. Spread hash mixture in skillet. Cook over medium heat until bottom is brown; sprinkle with

French fried onions. Bake uncovered until light brown, about 15 minutes. Top each serving with an egg.
4 OR 5 SERVINGS.

EGGS SUNNY-SIDE UP
Heat butter or bacon fat to ⅛-inch depth in heavy skillet just until hot enough to sizzle drop of water. Break each egg into a measuring cup or saucer; carefully slip 1 egg at a time into skillet. Immediately reduce heat. Cook slowly, spooning butter over eggs, until whites are set and a film forms over yolks.

Cut liver while bacon fries.

Drain bacon; cook onion.

Coat liver strips with flour.

Stir in tomatoes and corn.

Liver Fritada

4 slices bacon
1 medium onion, chopped (about ½ cup)
1 tablespoon flour
1 tablespoon chili powder
1 pound beef liver, cut into ¼-inch strips
1 can (16 ounces) whole tomatoes
1 can (12 ounces) whole kernel corn with
   sweet peppers
1 teaspoon salt
   Dash of pepper

Fry bacon in 12-inch skillet or Dutch oven until crisp; drain on paper towels. Crumble bacon and reserve. Drain fat from skillet, reserving 2 tablespoons. Return 2 tablespoons fat to skillet. Cook and stir onion in fat until tender, about 2 minutes.

Mix flour and chili powder. Coat liver with flour mixture; add to onion in skillet. Cook and stir until liver is light brown. Stir in tomatoes (with liquid), corn (with liquid), salt and pepper. Heat to boiling; reduce heat. Simmer uncovered until liver is tender, about 5 minutes. Sprinkle with reserved bacon.   4 SERVINGS.

KITCHEN AIDS

3 teaspoons = 1 tablespoon
16 tablespoons = 1 cup
2 cups = 1 pint
2 pints = 1 quart
4 quarts (liquid) = 1 gallon
28.35 grams = 1 ounce
16 ounces = 1 pound

Pork and Potato Stacks

1¾ cups hot water
1 package (6 ounces) hash brown
    potatoes with onions
6 pork cubed steaks (about 1½ pounds)
2 tablespoons shortening
½ teaspoon salt
1 cup shredded Cheddar cheese (about
    4 ounces)
1 carton (8 ounces) dairy sour cream
¼ cup milk
1 teaspoon salt
¼ teaspoon pepper
¼ teaspoon dried dill weed

Pour water on potatoes; let stand 10 minutes. Brown pork cubed steaks in shortening in two 10-inch skillets, about 7 minutes on each side. Sprinkle with ½ teaspoon salt; place on ungreased baking sheet.

Heat cheese in 2-quart saucepan over medium heat, stirring constantly, until melted. Stir in sour cream, milk, 1 teaspoon salt, the pepper and dill. Drain potatoes; stir into cheese mixture.

Set oven control to broil and/or 550°. Top each steak with ½ cup of the potato mixture. Broil with tops 3 inches from heat until potatoes are light brown, 3 to 4 minutes.
6 SERVINGS.

Brown steaks in two skillets.

Stir potatoes into the cheese.

Measure the potato mixture.

Invert mixture on hot steaks.

Add cut-up pork to the onion and celery in skillet.

Stir the flour-water mixture into the pork mixture.

Mandarin Pork Curry

    1 medium onion, sliced
    1 medium stalk celery, sliced (about
        ½ cup)
    2 tablespoons vegetable oil
    2 cups cut-up cooked pork
 1¼ cups water
    1 teaspoon instant chicken bouillon
    1 to 2 teaspoons curry powder
    ½ teaspoon salt
    2 tablespoons flour
    ¼ cup water
    1 can (11 ounces) mandarin orange
        segments, drained
      Hot cooked rice

Cook and stir onion and celery in oil in 10-inch skillet until onion is tender. Add pork, 1¼ cups water, the instant bouillon, curry powder and salt. Heat to boiling; remove from heat.

Blend flour and ¼ cup water; stir gradually into pork mixture. Heat to boiling, stirring constantly. Boil and stir 1 minute. Add orange segments and heat until oranges are hot. Serve over hot rice.   4 TO 6 SERVINGS.

Pork and Apple Curry: Substitute 1 medium apple, cut up, for the mandarin orange segments. Cook and stir with the onion and celery.

To make carrot curls, fasten long, thin strips with picks; crisp in cold water 3 hours.

To serve, remove picks; fill centers with olives, parsley sprigs or celery leaves.

Marmalade Ham

1½-pound fully cooked center smoked ham
    slice, about 1 inch thick
½ cup orange marmalade
1 teaspoon prepared horseradish
¼ teaspoon ground cloves
    Carrot curls

Heat oven to 325°. Place ham in ungreased baking dish, 11¾x7½x1¾ inches. Mix marmalade, horseradish and cloves; spread over ham. Bake until ham is hot, about 30 minutes. Garnish with carrot curls.   5 OR 6 SERVINGS.

Cranberry Ham: Reduce marmalade to ¼ cup and substitute ¼ cup cranberry-orange relish for the horseradish.

Broiled Ham Platter

1 can (24 ounces) fully cooked ham
  Whole cloves
1 can (11 ounces) mandarin orange
  segments, drained (reserve 2 tablespoons
  syrup)
½ teaspoon prepared horseradish
1 can (16 ounces) whole new potatoes,
  drained
1 can (16 ounces) whole green beans,
  drained
1 can (4 ounces) mushroom stems and
  pieces, drained
2 tablespoons butter or margarine, softened
⅛ teaspoon paprika
  Dried thyme leaves

Heat oven to 350°. Cut ham horizontally in half. Cut top of each half ¼ inch deep in 1-inch diamond pattern; insert cloves in cuts. Place in broiler pan. Mix reserved orange syrup and horseradish; drizzle over ham. Bake 10 minutes.

Arrange potatoes, beans and mushrooms around ham; place orange segments between ham slices. Dot vegetables with butter. Sprinkle potatoes with paprika, and beans and mushrooms with thyme.

Set oven control to broil and/or 550°. Broil with tops 4 to 5 inches from heat about 5 minutes.   4 OR 5 SERVINGS.

Ham 'n Cheese Stacks

1 package pie crust mix or sticks
¼ teaspoon dry mustard
1 small onion, chopped (about ¼ cup)
2 tablespoons chopped green pepper
2 tablespoons butter or margarine
1 can (10¾ ounces) condensed cream of
   mushroom soup
1 cup cut-up fully cooked ham
1 cup shredded Cheddar cheese (about
   4 ounces)
⅓ cup milk
½ teaspoon Worcestershire sauce
2 hard-cooked eggs, sliced

Heat oven to 450°. Prepare pastry for One-Crust Pie as
directed on package except—stir in mustard and roll into
rectangle, 12x9 inches. Cut into twelve 3-inch squares;

prick with fork. Place on ungreased baking sheet. Bake 6 to 8 minutes or until light brown.

Cook and stir onion and green pepper in butter until onion is tender. Stir in remaining ingredients; heat until bubbly. Arrange half of the pastry squares on plates. Spoon half of the ham mixture onto squares. Top with remaining squares. Spoon remaining ham mixture onto tops. Garnish with parsley.   6 SERVINGS.

Ham Rolls

1 package (10 ounces) frozen asparagus
   spears
8 thin slices fully cooked ham
1 can (10¾ ounces) condensed cream of
   shrimp soup
¼ cup dry white wine or water

Heat oven to 350°. Cook asparagus spears as directed on package; drain. Wrap each ham slice around 2 or 3 asparagus spears. Place in ungreased baking dish,10x6x1¾ inches. Mix soup and wine; pour on ham rolls. Bake uncovered until bubbly, 20 to 25 minutes.   4 SERVINGS.

Wrap each ham slice around 2 or 3 asparagus spears.

Pour the soup-wine mixture evenly on the Ham Rolls.

Slice frankfurters while the tomato mixture simmers.

Prepare Grilled Cheese Sandwiches while sauce simmers.

Grill the sandwiches until golden and cheese is melted.

Add water and cornstarch to franks; heat to boiling.

Mardi Gras Cheese and Franks

1 medium onion, sliced
1 small green pepper, chopped (about
   ½ cup)
2 tablespoons butter or margarine
1 can (16 ounces) whole tomatoes
1 teaspoon seasoned salt
1 teaspoon sugar
8 frankfurters, cut lengthwise in half
1 can (4 ounces) sliced mushrooms, drained
   Grilled Cheese Sandwiches (right)
¼ cup water
2 tablespoons cornstarch

Cook and stir onion and green pepper in butter in 3-quart saucepan over medium heat until onion is tender, about 3 minutes. Stir in tomatoes (with liquid), seasoned salt and sugar. Heat to boiling; reduce heat. Simmer uncovered 6 minutes. Stir in frankfurters and mushrooms. Simmer uncovered 12 minutes.

Prepare Grilled Cheese Sandwiches. Mix water and cornstarch; stir into frankfurter mixture. Cook, stirring constantly, until mixture thickens and boils. Boil and stir 1 minute. Top each sandwich with 2 frankfurter halves and about ¼ cup of the sauce.   8 SERVINGS.

GRILLED CHEESE SANDWICHES

Heat griddle or two 12-inch skillets over medium heat. Spread butter or margarine, softened, over 1 side of each of 8 slices bread. Place bread buttered sides down on hot griddle. Top with 8 slices cheese. Top cheese with 8 slices bread. Spread butter over bread. Grill sandwiches on both sides until cheese is melted and sandwiches are golden brown.

Frank Fiesta

- 8 to 10 frankfurters, cut into ½-inch slices
- 1 medium onion, chopped (about ½ cup)
- 1 tablespoon vegetable oil
- 1 can (15 ounces) tomato sauce
- 1 can (8 ounces) whole kernel corn
- 1 can (8 ounces) kidney beans
- 5 ounces uncooked spiral macaroni or noodles
- ½ cup water
- 1½ to 2 teaspoons chili powder
- 1 teaspoon salt
- ½ medium green pepper, cut into strips

Cook and stir frankfurter slices and onion in oil in 12-inch skillet or Dutch oven until frankfurters are light brown and onion is tender. Stir in remaining ingredients except green pepper. Heat to boiling; reduce heat. Cover and simmer, stirring occasionally, until macaroni is tender, 20 to 25 minutes.

Add green pepper. Cover and simmer until green pepper is crisp-tender, about 5 minutes.   4 TO 6 SERVINGS.

Swiss Salad

1 package (8 ounces) summer sausage, cut
   into ¼-inch strips
½ cup mayonnaise or salad dressing
1 teaspoon prepared mustard
1 can (16 ounces) sauerkraut, drained and
   cut through with scissors
1 jar (2 ounces) sliced pimiento, drained
2 medium stalks celery, sliced (about 1 cup)
4 ounces Swiss cheese, cut into cubes
1 small onion, sliced

Reserve ½ cup summer sausage strips. Mix mayonnaise
and mustard in large bowl. Stir in sauerkraut, remaining
sausage, pimiento, celery and cheese; toss. Garnish with
onion slices and reserved summer sausage.   6 SERVINGS.

MUSTARD adds zest to many foods. Use the seeds for pickling, garnishes or barbecue sauce. Spreadable prepared mustard comes in several varieties, including horseradish and wine-flavored. Dry mustard is more concentrated than prepared mustard. 1 teaspoon dry equals 1 or 2 tablespoons prepared.

Cook the spaghetti while the sauce simmers.

Stir the corn and sliced olives into the sauce.

Pizzaghetti

1 pound mild Italian bulk sausage
1 tablespoon vegetable oil
1 can (16 ounces) stewed tomatoes
1 can (8 ounces) tomato sauce
½ teaspoon dried basil leaves, crushed
½ teaspoon salt
¼ teaspoon garlic powder
¼ teaspoon pepper
7 ounces uncooked spaghetti
1 can (12 ounces) whole kernel corn with
    sweet peppers
⅓ cup sliced pimiento-stuffed olives
5 thin slices mozzarella or Monterey Jack
    cheese

Cook and stir Italian bulk sausage in oil in 10-inch skillet over medium heat until light brown, about 6 minutes; drain. Stir in tomatoes, tomato sauce, basil, salt, garlic powder and pepper. Heat to boiling; reduce heat. Simmer uncovered, stirring occasionally, 10 minutes.

Cook spaghetti as directed on package; drain. Stir corn (with liquid) and olives into sausage mixture. Simmer uncovered 5 minutes. Serve over spaghetti; top each serving with a cheese slice.   5 SERVINGS.

Brown pork luncheon meat in skillet, stirring occasionally.

Stir in mayonnaise, vinegar, onion, mustard, vegetables.

Shoestring Salad

1 can (7 ounces) pork luncheon meat, cut into ¼-inch cubes
½ cup mayonnaise or salad dressing
1 to 2 tablespoons vinegar
1 tablespoon instant minced onion
1 teaspoon prepared mustard
1 can (8½ ounces) mixed vegetables, drained
1 can (1½ ounces) shoestring potatoes
3 tablespoons grated Parmesan cheese

Brown pork luncheon meat in 10-inch skillet over medium heat, stirring occasionally. Remove from heat; drain. Stir in mayonnaise, vinegar, onion, mustard and mixed vegetables; toss. Just before serving, fold in potatoes and sprinkle with cheese. Serve hot.   3 OR 4 SERVINGS.

Veal Chop Suey

1 pound veal round steak, cut into ½-inch
   cubes
1 medium onion, thinly sliced
2 large stalks celery, cut diagonally into
   slices (about 1½ cups)
2 tablespoons vegetable oil
1 can (16 ounces) bean sprouts, drained
1¾ cups water
1 teaspoon salt
3 tablespoons cornstarch
3 tablespoons cold water
3 tablespoons soy sauce
1 teaspoon packed brown sugar
1 jar (2½ ounces) sliced mushrooms,
   drained
1 cup cherry tomatoes, cut in half
   Chow mein noodles

Cook and stir veal cubes, onion and celery in oil in 10-inch
skillet over medium heat until veal is brown and onion is
tender, about 5 minutes. Stir in bean sprouts, 1¾ cups
water and the salt. Heat to boiling; reduce heat. Cover and
simmer until veal is tender, about 15 minutes.

Mix cornstarch, 3 tablespoons cold water, the soy sauce
and brown sugar; stir into veal mixture. Cook, stirring constantly, until mixture thickens and boils. Boil and stir 1
minute. Stir in mushrooms; fold in tomatoes. Serve over
chow mein noodles.   4 SERVINGS.

Start veal; slice mushrooms.

Simmer veal; cook noodles.

Mix soup and milk; add to veal.

Toss noodles, butter and seed.

Veal Strips Stroganoff

1 pound veal round steak, ¼ inch thick, cut
  into ¼-inch strips
¼ cup butter or margarine
¼ teaspoon salt
⅛ teaspoon dried thyme leaves
⅛ teaspoon pepper
½ pound mushrooms, sliced
¼ cup frozen chopped onion (optional)
¼ cup water
5 ounces uncooked noodles (about 2⅔ cups)
1 can (10¾ ounces) condensed cream of
  mushroom soup
½ cup milk
1 tablespoon butter or margarine
1 teaspoon poppy seed

Cook veal strips in ¼ cup butter in 10-inch skillet over
medium heat, stirring occasionally, until light brown,
about 3 minutes. Sprinkle veal with salt, thyme and pepper. Stir in mushrooms, onion and water. Heat to boiling;
reduce heat. Cover and simmer until veal is tender, about
20 minutes.

Cook noodles as directed on package. Mix soup and milk;
stir into veal mixture. Heat until soup is hot. Drain noodles;
toss with 1 tablespoon butter and the poppy seed. Serve
stroganoff over noodles.   4 SERVINGS.

Mandarin Lamb

1½ pounds lean lamb boneless shoulder, cut
    into ½-inch strips
¼ teaspoon garlic powder
2 tablespoons butter or margarine
1 medium onion, chopped (about ½ cup)
1 cup water
1½ cups water
½ teaspoon salt
1 cup uncooked instant brown rice
¼ cup water
3 tablespoons soy sauce
2 tablespoons cornstarch
½ teaspoon salt
¼ teaspoon pepper
1 medium green pepper, cut into rings
1 can (11 ounces) mandarin orange
    segments, drained

Cook and stir lamb strips and garlic powder in butter in
10-inch skillet until lamb is brown, about 6 minutes. Stir in
onion and 1 cup water. Heat to boiling; reduce heat. Cover
and simmer 15 minutes.

Heat 1½ cups water and ½ teaspoon salt to boiling in
1½-quart saucepan. Stir in rice; reduce heat. Cover and
steam 15 minutes.

Mix ¼ cup water, the soy sauce, cornstarch, ½ teaspoon
salt and the pepper; stir into lamb mixture. Add green
pepper rings, reserving 2 or 3 rings for garnish. Cook, stirring constantly, until mixture thickens and boils. Boil and
stir 1 minute. Fold in orange segments. Serve over rice and
garnish with reserved green pepper rings.   4 SERVINGS.

Chop the onion while the lamb and the garlic brown.

Prepare the rice; let stand. Cut the pepper rings.

Stir soy sauce mixture into lamb; add pepper rings.

Fold in mandarin orange segments; garnish with pepper.

Chicken in Potato Boats

2 cups cut-up cooked chicken
1 medium stalk celery, sliced (about ½ cup)
¼ cup pitted ripe olives
1 tablespoon chopped pimiento
½ teaspoon chili powder
¼ cup dairy sour cream
1 can (10¾ ounces) condensed cream of
   chicken soup
½ cup instant mashed potato puffs
3 tablespoons butter or margarine
   Potato Boats (right)
¾ cup dairy sour cream
¼ teaspoon salt

Heat oven to 350°. Mix chicken, celery, olives, pimiento, chili powder, ¼ cup sour cream and ½ cup of the soup; reserve. Cook and stir potato puffs in butter until golden; reserve for topping.

Prepare Potato Boats. Spoon chicken mixture into Potato Boats. Sprinkle with browned potato puffs. Bake 30 minutes.

Mix remaining soup, ¾ cup sour cream and the salt. Heat just to boiling. Serve over chicken.   8 SERVINGS.

POTATO BOATS

Prepare instant mashed potato puffs for 8 servings as directed on package except—reduce water to 2 cups. Stir in 1 egg, slightly beaten, and ¼ cup grated American cheese food. Spoon into 8 mounds on greased baking sheet. Hollow centers with the back of a spoon.

Ahead of time, prepare chicken filling and brown ½ cup potato puffs. Cook remaining potato puffs; divide into 8 equal parts.

Spoon potatoes into 8 mounds; hollow centers, fill and sprinkle with potato puffs. Heat soup and sour cream for the sauce.

Heat chicken and shrimp mixture, stirring occasionally.

Stir in chives and pimiento; spoon into baked patty shells.

Chicken and Mushroom Shells

2 packages (6 each) frozen patty shells
2 cups chicken broth
3 tablespoons cornstarch
1 package (8 ounces) cream cheese, softened
1 can (13 ounces) evaporated milk
3 cups cut-up cooked chicken or turkey
1 can (about 4½ ounces) small shrimp, drained
1 can (4½ ounces) sliced mushrooms
2 to 4 tablespoons snipped chives
2 tablespoons chopped pimiento
Paprika

Prepare patty shells as directed on package. Stir broth gradually into cornstarch in 2-quart saucepan. Add cheese and milk. Heat to boiling, stirring constantly. Boil and stir 1 minute. Stir in chicken, shrimp and mushrooms (with liquid). Heat until chicken and shrimp are hot.

Stir in chives and pimiento. Spoon about ⅔ cup of the chicken mixture into each patty shell. Sprinkle with paprika and garnish with snipped parsley.   12 SERVINGS.

TAKE STOCK

A handy way to freeze chicken or meat stock is to pour it into ice cube trays, then remove frozen cubes and pack in plastic bags. Store in freezer up to 6 months at 0°.

Freeze cooked poultry in recipe-size quantities. Cut up and pack tightly in freezer containers with or without the broth. Cooked poultry without broth can be frozen up to 1 month; with broth up to 6 months. Thaw in refrigerator up to 24 hours before using.

Chicken over Corn Bread

Corn Bread (below)
1 package (10 ounces) frozen chopped broccoli
1 tablespoon finely chopped onion
1 clove garlic, finely chopped
¼ cup butter or margarine
2 tablespoons flour
1½ teaspoons salt
¾ cup milk
2 egg yolks, slightly beaten
1 carton (8 ounces) unflavored yogurt
1 can (5 ounces) boned chicken, broken
  into chunks
¼ cup shredded Cheddar cheese

Bake Corn Bread. Rinse frozen broccoli under running cold water to separate. Cook and stir broccoli, onion and garlic in butter in 10-inch skillet over low heat 5 minutes; remove from heat. Blend in flour and salt. Cook, stirring constantly, until bubbly; remove from heat. Stir in milk. Heat to boiling, stirring constantly. Boil and stir 1 minute.

Mix egg yolks and yogurt. Stir yogurt mixture and chicken chunks into broccoli mixture. Heat over low heat, stirring frequently, until chicken is hot; serve over Corn Bread. Sprinkle with cheese.   6 SERVINGS.

CORN BREAD

2 eggs
1 cup biscuit baking mix
1 cup cornmeal
1½ cups buttermilk
2 tablespoons vegetable oil
½ teaspoon poultry seasoning

Heat oven to 450°. Grease baking pan, 9x9x2 inches. Beat eggs until fluffy; beat in remaining ingredients just until smooth. Bake until golden brown, 25 minutes.

Blend flour and salt into broccoli mixture in skillet.

After cooking mixture, remove from heat; stir in milk.

To make corn bread, grease pan generously.

Beat eggs; beat in remaining ingredients until smooth.

Little Chicken Pies

1 can (10¾ ounces) condensed cream of
  chicken soup
1 can (8 ounces) green peas, drained
1 can (5 ounces) boned chicken, broken into
  chunks
1 can (4 ounces) mushroom stems and
  pieces
¼ teaspoon poultry seasoning
1 cup biscuit baking mix
⅓ cup milk
¼ cup broken pecans
  Paprika

Heat oven to 425°. Heat soup, peas, chicken, mushrooms
(with liquid) and poultry seasoning to boiling over medium
heat, stirring occasionally. Stir baking mix, milk and pecans until a soft dough forms; beat vigorously 20 strokes.

Spoon chicken mixture into 4 greased 10-ounce casseroles;
top each with ¼ of the biscuit dough. Bake uncovered until
biscuits are golden brown, 20 to 25 minutes. Sprinkle with
paprika. 4 SERVINGS.

Spoon the chicken mixture into
4 individual casseroles.

Top each casserole with ¼ of
the biscuit dough; bake.

Holiday Sandwiches

1 cup biscuit baking mix
¼ cup cold water
5 slices cooked turkey (about 6x2 inches)
5 thin slices Swiss cheese (about 6x2 inches)
5 slices cooked ham (about 6x2 inches)
1 package (about 1 ounce) chicken gravy
   mix
¼ cup dry white wine
1 can (4 ounces) mushroom stems and
   pieces, drained

Heat oven to 450°. Mix baking mix and water; beat vigorously 20 strokes. Pat into rectangle, 10x5 inches, on ungreased baking sheet. Cut rectangle crosswise into five 2-inch strips, but do not separate. Bake until strips are golden brown, about 10 minutes.

Set oven control to broil and/or 550°. Separate biscuit strips; place slice of turkey, cheese and ham on each strip. Broil with tops 5 inches from heat until cheese is melted, about 4 minutes.

Prepare gravy mix as directed on package except—substitute the wine for ¼ cup of the water; stir in mushrooms. Serve gravy over sandwiches.   5 SERVINGS.

Party Chicken Livers

1 pound chicken livers, cut into 1-inch
    pieces
¼ cup butter or margarine
    Toast Cups (below)
1 can (10¾ ounces) condensed cream of
    mushroom soup
1 can (8½ ounces) water chestnuts, drained
    and sliced
2 tablespoons chopped pimiento
¼ teaspoon salt
½ cup canned French fried onions

Cook and stir chicken livers in butter over medium heat until livers are brown, about 12 minutes. Prepare Toast Cups. Stir soup, water chestnuts, pimiento and salt into livers. Heat until mixture is hot and bubbly, about 1 minute. Serve in Toast Cups. Top with onions.

6 SERVINGS.

TOAST CUPS

Heat oven to 375°. Trim crusts from 6 slices thinly sliced bread. Spread butter or margarine, softened, over 1 side of each slice. Press bread buttered sides down in ungreased medium muffin cups. Bake until lightly toasted, about 12 minutes.

Trim crust from bread; spread with butter. Press into cups.

Prepare chicken livers; serve in Toast Cups. Top with onions.

Season cut halibut; broil 1 side.

Cook potato puffs in butter.

Add tomatoes; turn the fish.

Heat Shrimp Sauce until hot.

Halibut with Shrimp Sauce

2 pounds halibut steaks
Salt
Pepper
Paprika
⅓ cup instant mashed potato puffs
3 tablespoons butter or margarine
⅛ teaspoon garlic powder
3 large tomatoes, cut in half
Shrimp Sauce (right)

Set oven control to broil and/or 550°. Cut halibut steaks into 6 serving pieces; sprinkle with salt, pepper and paprika. Broil with tops 3 inches from heat until light brown, 5 to 8 minutes.

Cook and stir potato puffs in butter and garlic powder until golden; sprinkle over tomato halves. Place tomatoes on broiler pan with halibut. Turn halibut; sprinkle with salt, pepper and paprika. Broil until halibut flakes easily with fork, 5 to 8 minutes. (Broiling time varies according to thickness of halibut.) Serve with Shrimp Sauce.
6 SERVINGS.

SHRIMP SAUCE

Heat 1 can (10¾ ounces) condensed cream of shrimp soup, 1 can (4½ ounces) broken shrimp, drained, and ¼ teaspoon dried dill weed over medium heat, stirring constantly, until hot and bubbly.

Tuna Short Pie

---

2 cans (6½ ounces each) tuna, drained and
   flaked
1 package (10 ounces) frozen chopped
   broccoli, thawed and drained
2 medium stalks celery, sliced (about 1 cup)
1 can (11 ounces) condensed Cheddar
   cheese soup
2 tablespoons milk
½ teaspoon onion salt
½ teaspoon dried marjoram leaves
   Biscuit Rounds (right)

54

Heat oven to 400°. Layer tuna, broccoli and celery in ungreased baking dish, 8x8x2 inches. Mix soup, milk, onion salt and marjoram; pour on tuna and vegetables. Heat in oven 15 minutes. While tuna mixture is heating, prepare Biscuits Rounds.

Overlap the Biscuit Rounds on tuna mixture. Bake uncovered until Biscuit Rounds are golden, 15 to 20 minutes. 6 SERVINGS.

BISCUIT ROUNDS

1 cup biscuit baking mix
¼ cup butter or margarine, softened
3 tablespoons boiling water

Combine baking mix and butter. Stir in water with fork until dough forms a ball and cleans side of bowl. (Dough will be puffy and soft.) Divide into 6 parts; flatten each into 3- to 4-inch round.

Salmon Short Pie: Substitute 1 can (16 ounces) salmon for the tuna. Flake salmon, removing skin and bones.

Layer tuna, broccoli and celery in baking dish.

Overlap Biscuit Rounds on soup mixture.

For boats, scoop seeds and membrane from pepper halves.

Fill peppers with the shrimp mixture. Garnish with parsley.

Shrimp Boats

1 package (10 ounces) frozen green peas
1 can (8½ ounces) whole new potatoes,
    drained and chopped
1 can (4½ ounces) tiny deveined shrimp,
    rinsed and drained
1 medium stalk celery, coarsely chopped
    (about ½ cup)
3 or 4 small sweet pickles, thinly sliced
½ cup shredded Cheddar cheese (2 ounces)
⅓ cup mayonnaise or salad dressing
2 teaspoons lemon juice
¾ teaspoon seasoned salt
3 large green peppers, cut lengthwise in half
    Lettuce leaves

Rinse frozen peas under running cold water to separate. Toss peas, potatoes, shrimp, celery, pickles, cheese, mayonnaise, lemon juice and seasoned salt. Scoop seeds and membrane from pepper halves; place halves on lettuce leaves. Fill peppers with shrimp mixture. Garnish with parsley.   6 SERVINGS.

KNOW THE DIFFERENCE

Grated cheese is dry, almost powdery cheese that has been put through the small holes of a grater. Cheese that has become dry and hard can be grated and stored in a covered container, or you can purchase grated cheese in shaker-top cans.

Shredded cheese is moist, fresh cheese put through the small holes of a shredder. You can shred it yourself or buy it in packages at most stores.

Impromptu Party Seafood

Crunchy Rice Ring (right)
2 cans (10¾ ounces each) condensed cream
   of shrimp soup
3 cans (4½ ounces each) deveined small
   shrimp, rinsed and drained*
1 can (6½ ounces) tuna, drained and broken
   into chunks
1 jar (2 ounces) sliced pimiento, drained
¼ cup apple cider

Prepare Crunchy Rice Ring. Heat soup, shrimp, tuna, pimiento and cider just to boiling in 2-quart saucepan over medium heat, stirring occasionally. Serve with Crunchy Rice Ring.   8 TO 10 SERVINGS.

*1 can (7 ounces) fish flakes can be substituted for 1 can of the shrimp.

CRUNCHY RICE RING

4½ cups water
2 cups uncooked regular rice
2 tablespoons butter or margarine
2 teaspoons salt
1 can (8 ounces) water chestnuts, drained
    and sliced

Heat water to boiling in 2-quart saucepan. Stir in rice, butter and salt; reduce heat. Cover and simmer until water is absorbed, about 25 minutes.

Stir in water chestnuts. Grease 6-cup ring mold or coat with vegetable spray-on for cookware. Pack rice mixture lightly in mold. Let stand 2 minutes. Unmold on serving platter.

To make rice ring, pack rice mixture lightly in greased mold; let stand 2 minutes.

Cover mold with serving platter. Invert, then lift off mold. Serve with hot seafood.

Creamy Ham and Eggs

1½ cups cubed cooked ham
½ medium green pepper, sliced
2 tablespoons butter or margarine
1 can (10¾ ounces) condensed cream
  of celery soup
½ cup milk
½ cup dairy sour cream
1 to 2 teaspoons prepared horseradish
1 teaspoon Worcestershire sauce
  Dash of pepper
4 hard-cooked eggs, cut into eighths
¼ cup chopped pimiento
  Hot buttered toast
  Paprika

Cook and stir ham and green pepper in butter in 10-inch skillet over medium heat until green pepper is crisp-tender, 2 to 3 minutes.

Mix soup, milk, sour cream, horseradish, Worcestershire sauce and pepper; stir into ham and green pepper. Heat to boiling; reduce heat. Simmer uncovered, stirring occasionally, 3 minutes. Stir in eggs and pimiento. Heat until eggs are hot. Serve over toast; sprinkle with paprika.
4 SERVINGS.

Cook ham and green pepper.

Cut the eggs into eighths.

Cook the vegetables while the eggs are beating.

Cook the egg puffs while the sauce simmers.

Cheese and Egg Puffs

6 eggs
1 medium green pepper, chopped (about 1 cup)
1 medium onion, chopped (about ½ cup)
2 tablespoons butter or margarine
2 teaspoons cornstarch
1 can (15 ounces) tomato sauce
1 can (4 ounces) sliced mushrooms, drained
¾ cup all-purpose flour
1½ teaspoons baking powder
½ teaspoon salt
1½ cups shredded Cheddar cheese (about 6 ounces)

Beat eggs in large mixer bowl until very thick and lemon colored, about 10 minutes. Cook and stir green pepper and onion in butter in 2-quart saucepan over medium heat until tender, about 2 minutes. Stir in cornstarch; add tomato sauce and mushrooms. Cook, stirring constantly, until mixture thickens; reduce heat. Cover and simmer 15 minutes.

Heat lightly greased griddle over medium heat. Mix flour, baking powder and salt; beat into eggs gradually. Fold in cheese. Drop batter by ¼ cupfuls onto hot griddle. Cook until light brown, about 2 minutes on each side. For each serving, top 2 egg puffs with ½ cup of the sauce.
6 SERVINGS.

Fruit-topped Oven Pancakes

Fruit Topping (below)
3 eggs
½ teaspoon salt
½ cup all-purpose flour*
½ cup milk
2 tablespoons butter or margarine
1½ cups shredded Cheddar or Swiss cheese
(about 6 ounces)
Powdered sugar

Heat oven to 450°. Prepare Fruit Topping. Place 2 round layer pans, 8x1½ inches, in oven. Beat eggs and salt in small mixer bowl on high speed 1 minute. Beat on low speed, adding flour and milk alternately in 3 additions; continue beating 1 minute.

Remove pans from oven. Place 1 tablespoon butter in each pan; brush pans with butter. Divide batter equally between pans. Bake uncovered 15 minutes. Reduce oven temperature to 350°. Bake 5 minutes.

Place pancakes on 2 warm serving plates; sprinkle with cheese. Spoon topping onto each pancake; sprinkle with sugar. Cut into wedges.   4 SERVINGS.

*Do not use self-rising flour in this recipe.

FRUIT TOPPING
Squeeze juice of ½ medium lemon over 2 cups sweetened sliced fresh fruit or berries.